This book belongs to

....

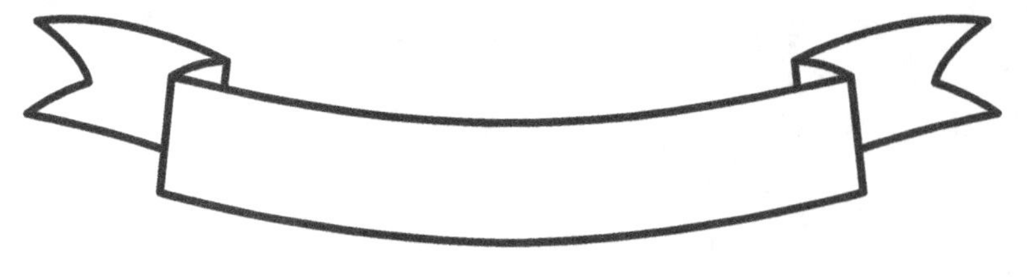

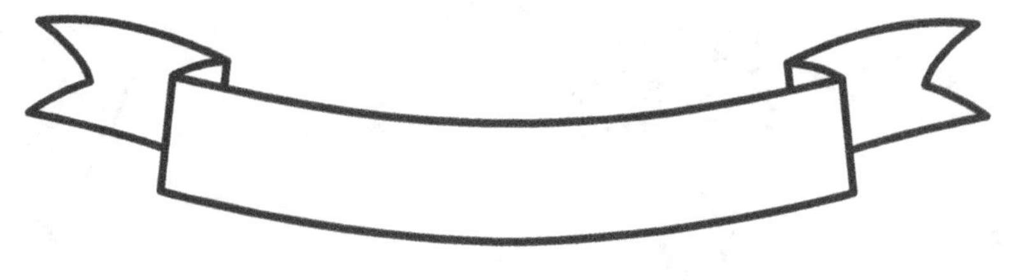

MILK
XOXO

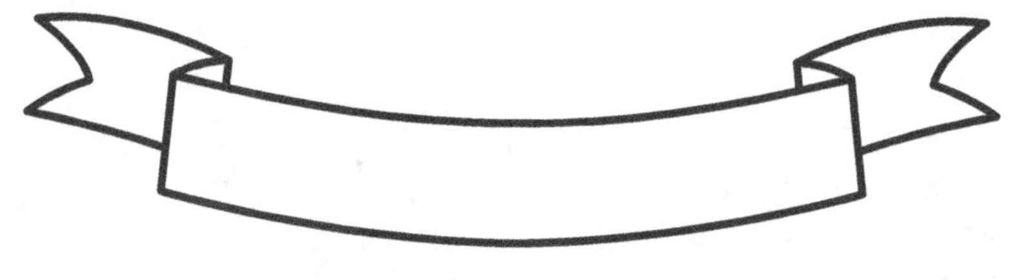

magic
Set
2

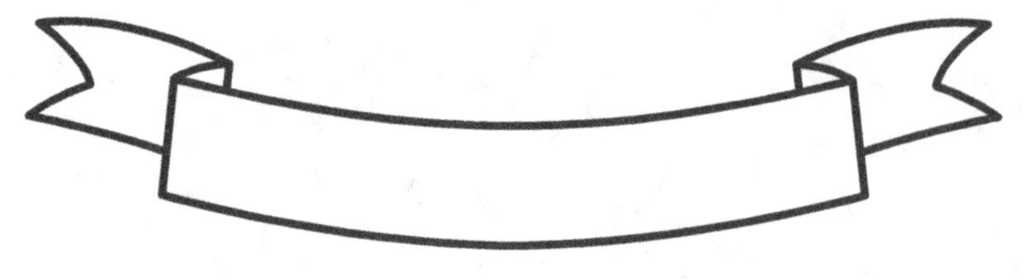

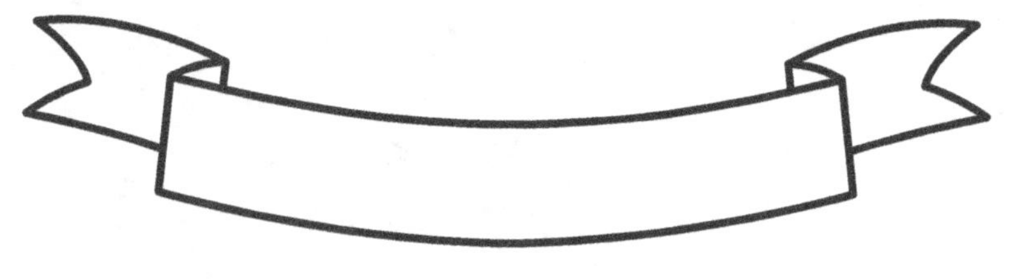

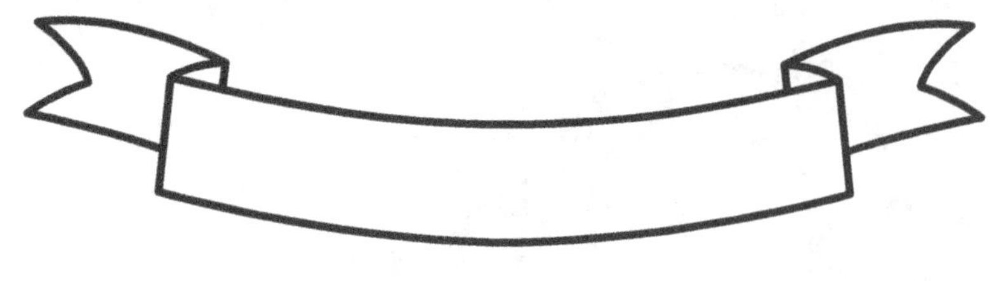

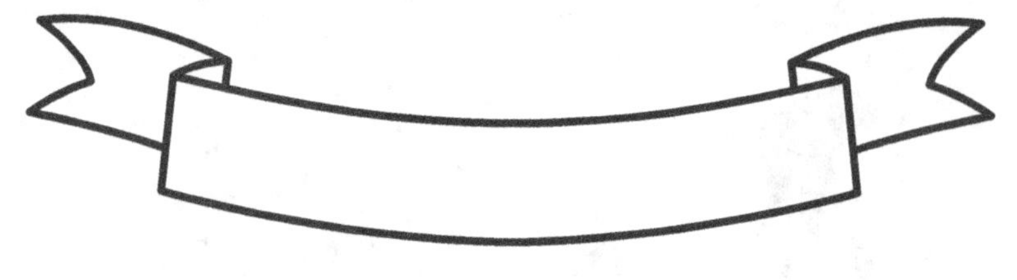

fairy tale

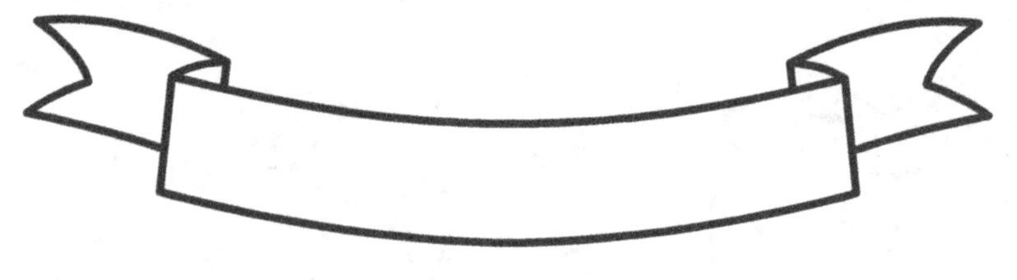

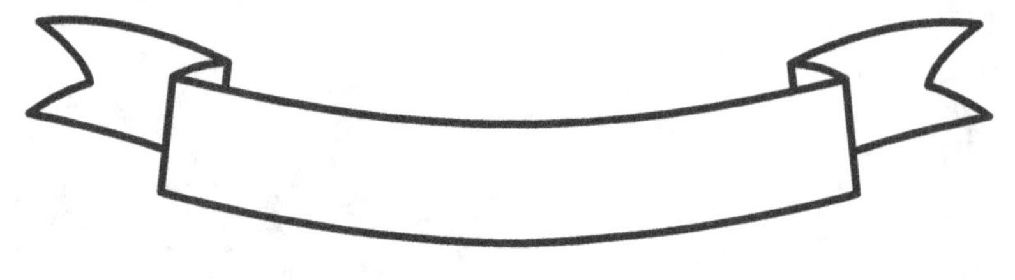

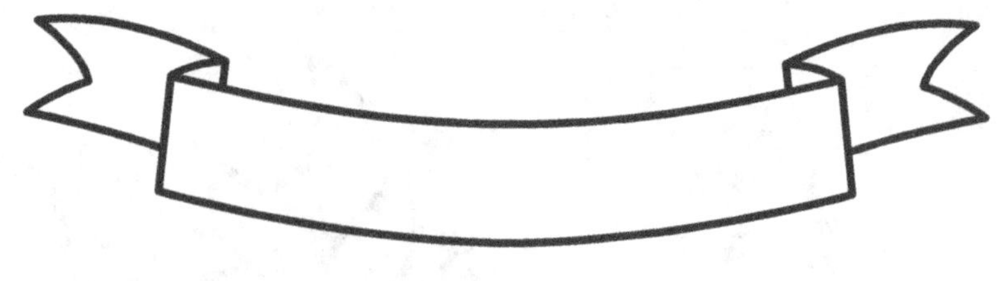

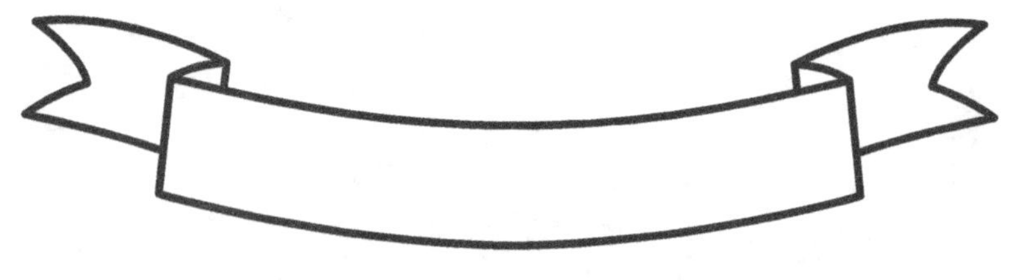

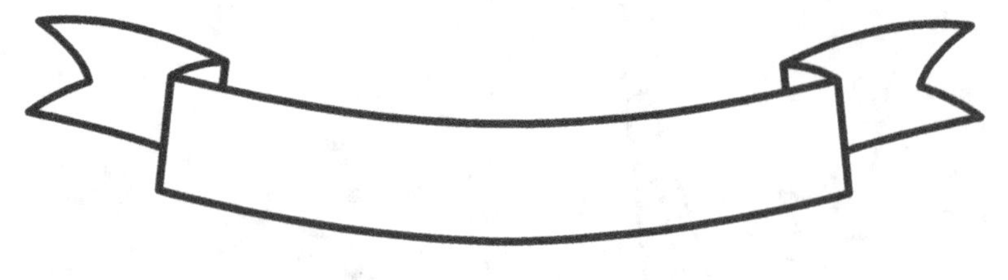

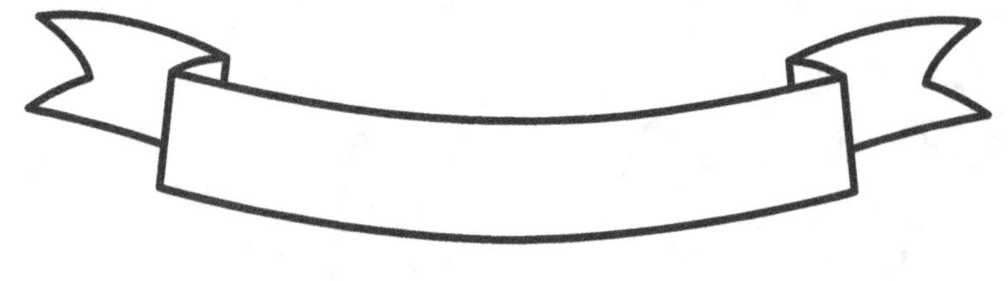

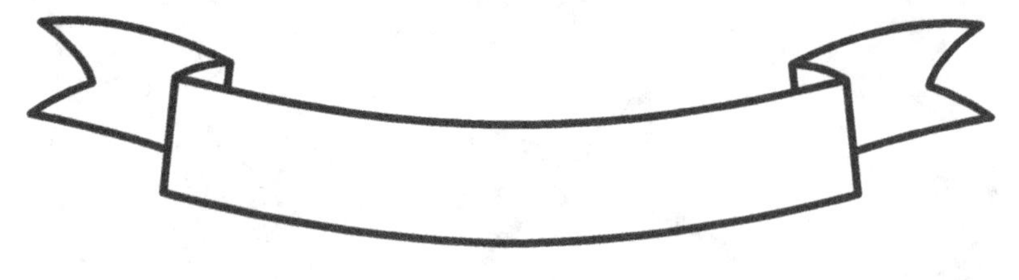

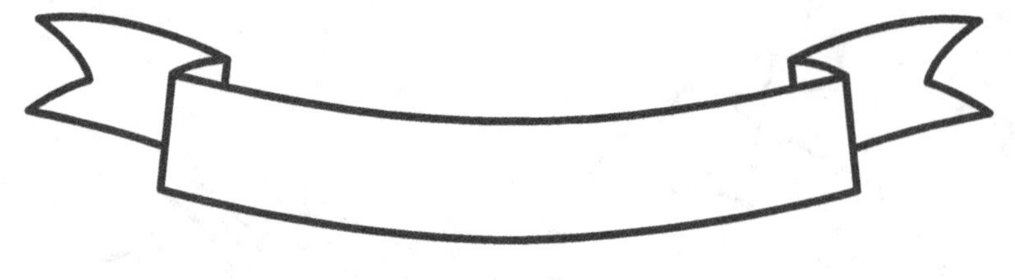

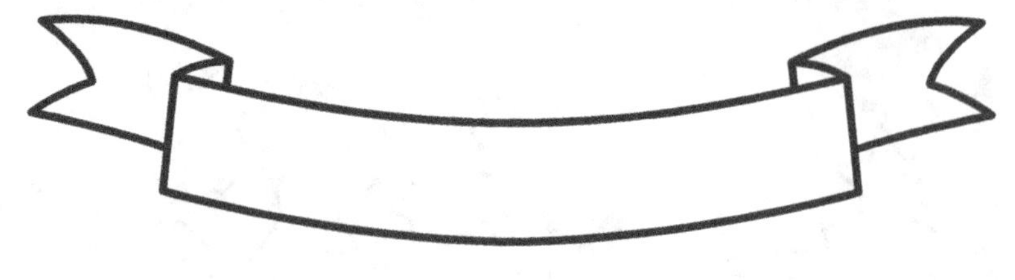

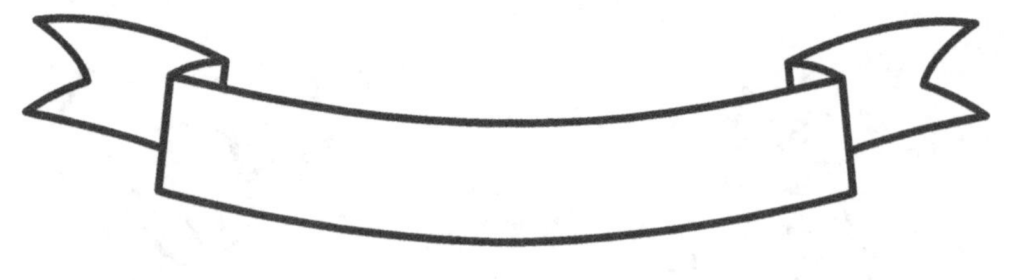

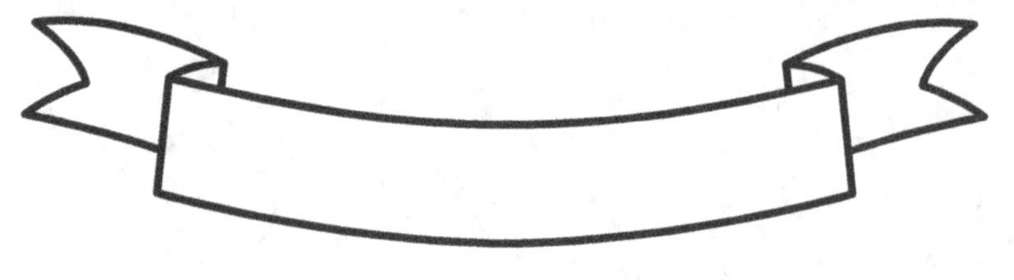

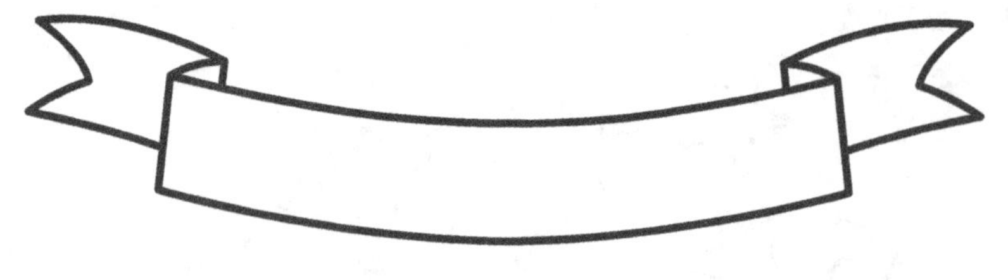

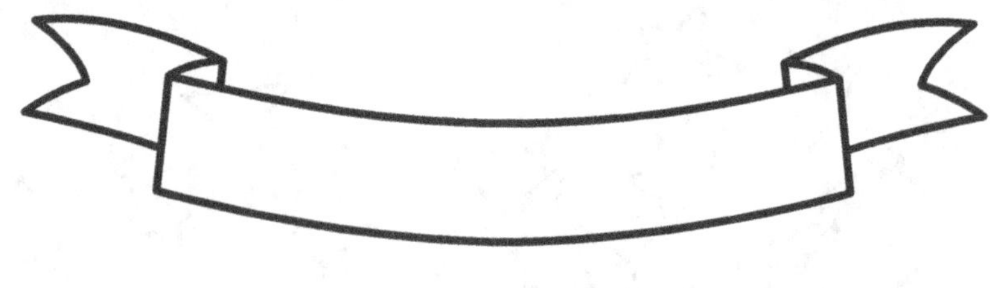

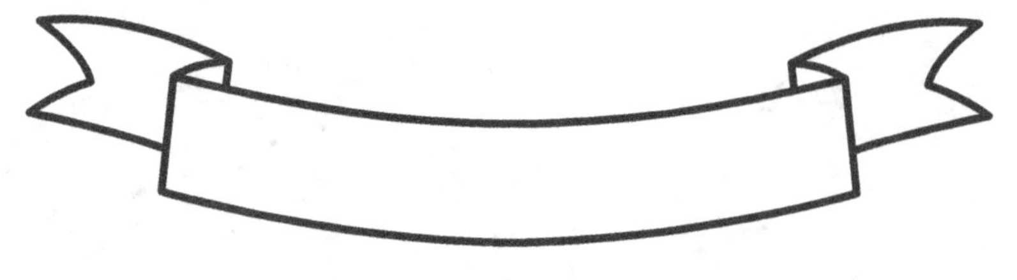

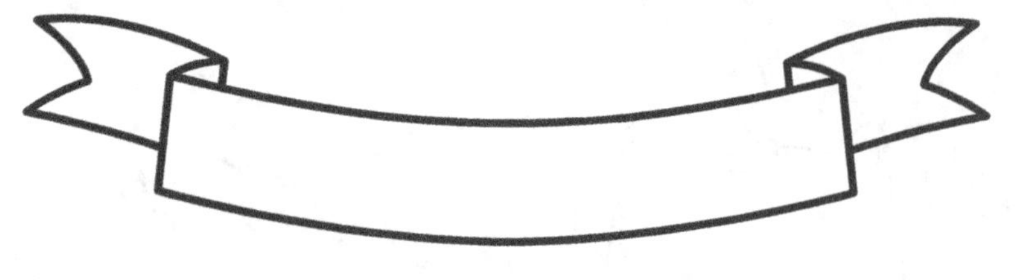

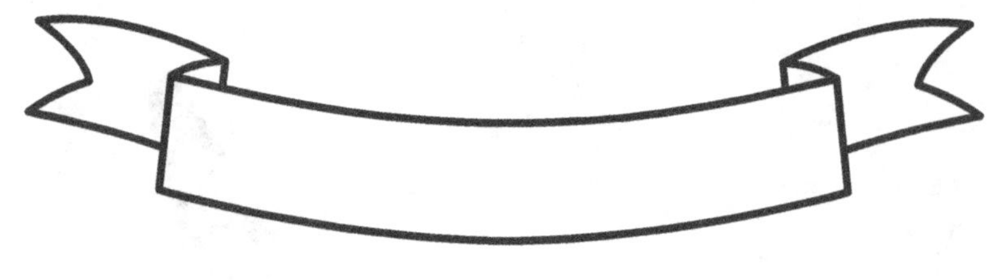

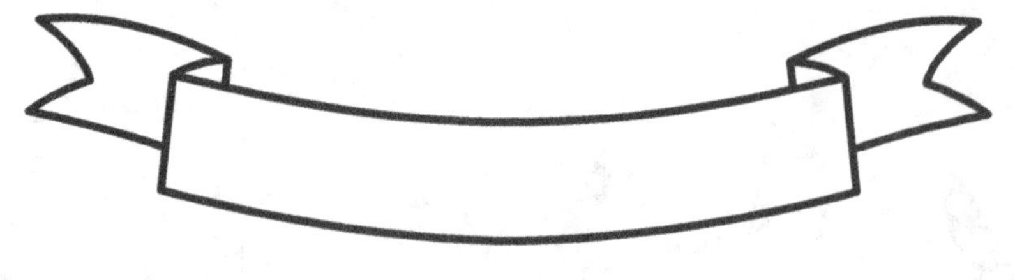

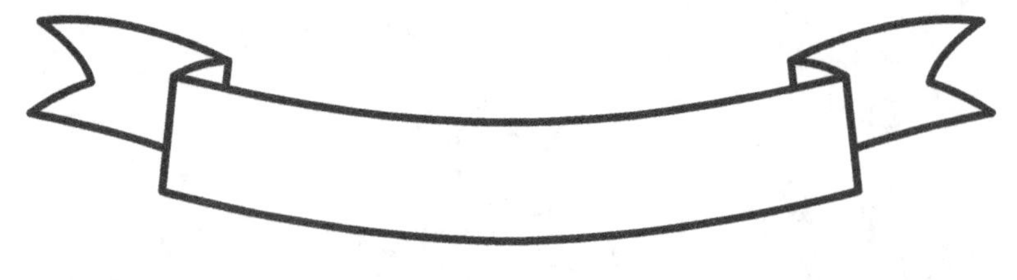

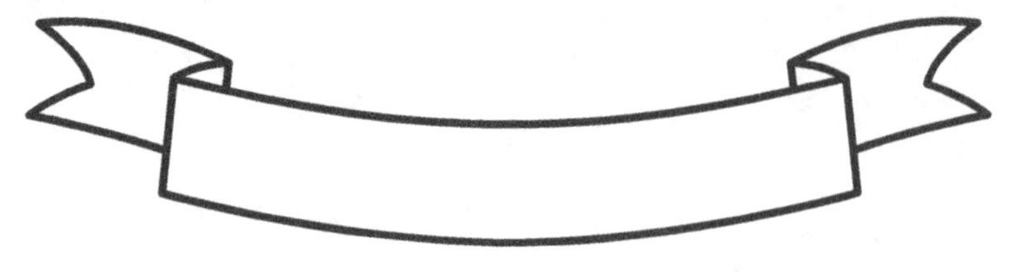

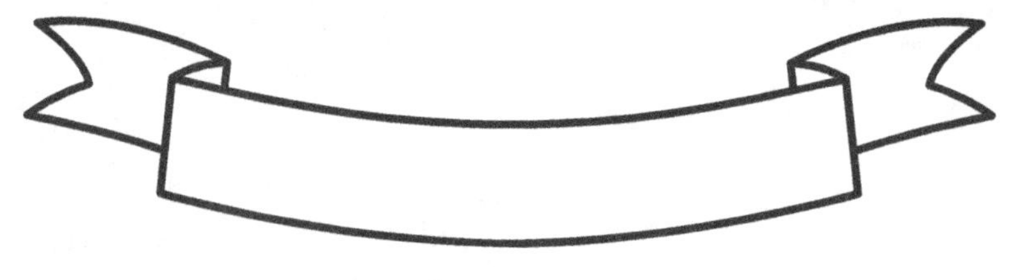

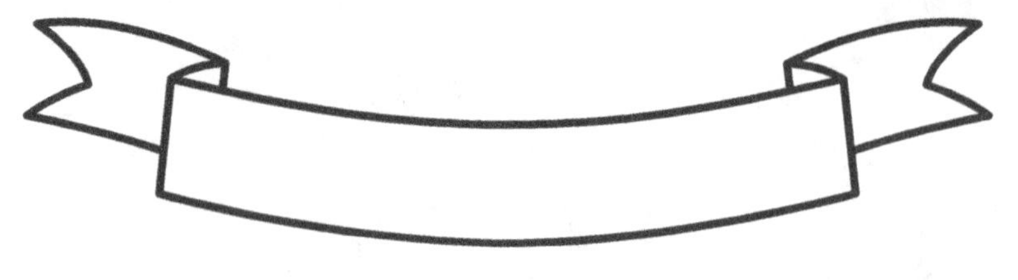

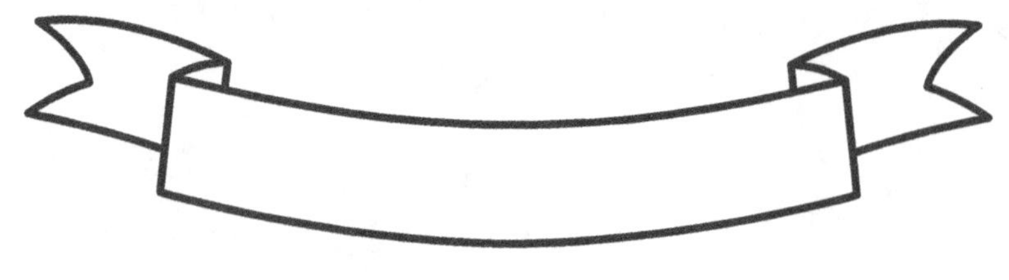

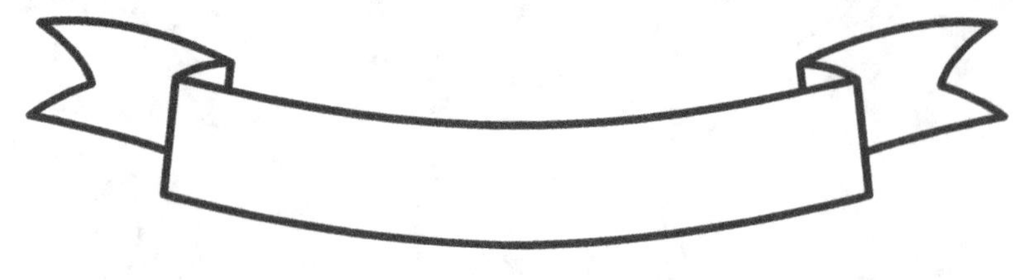

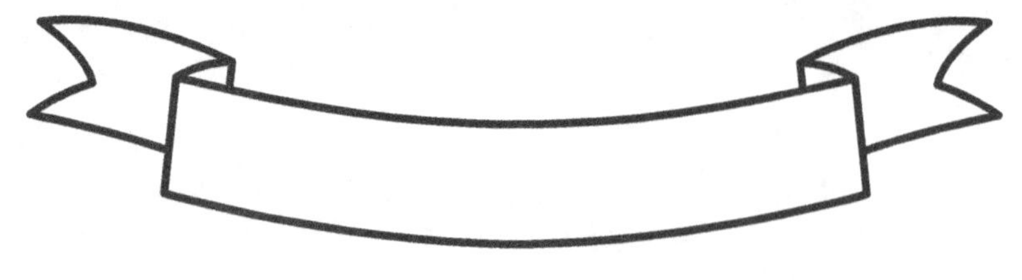

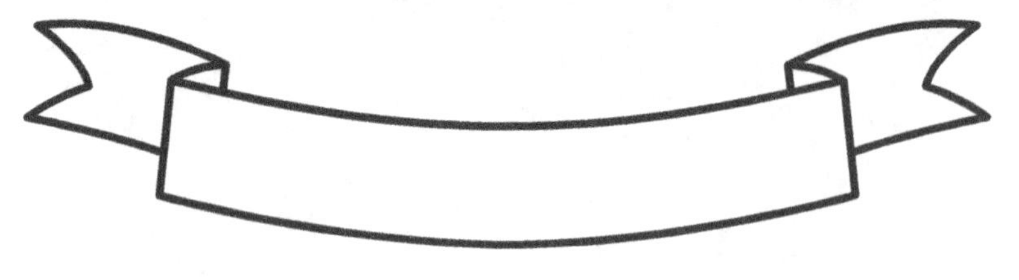

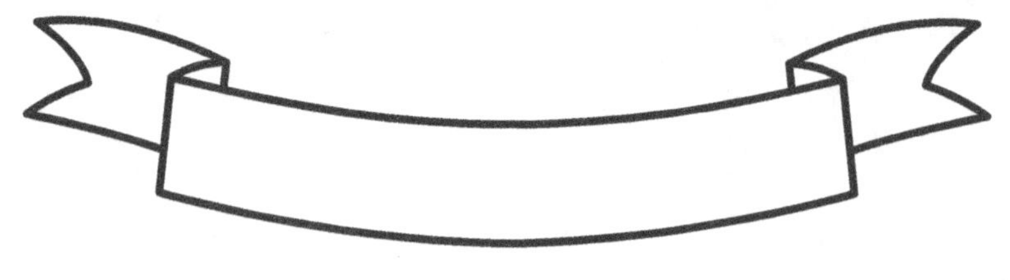

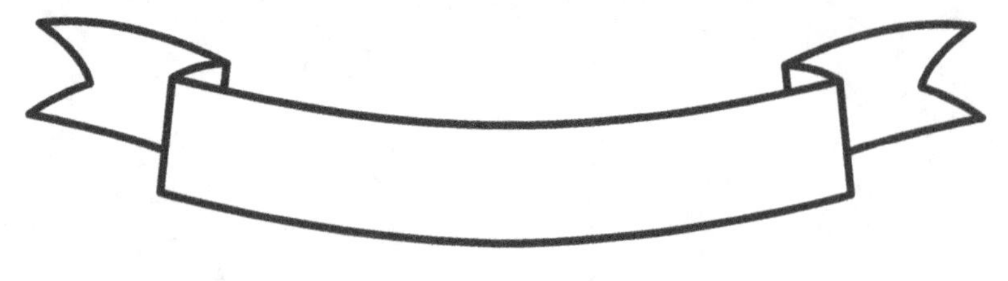

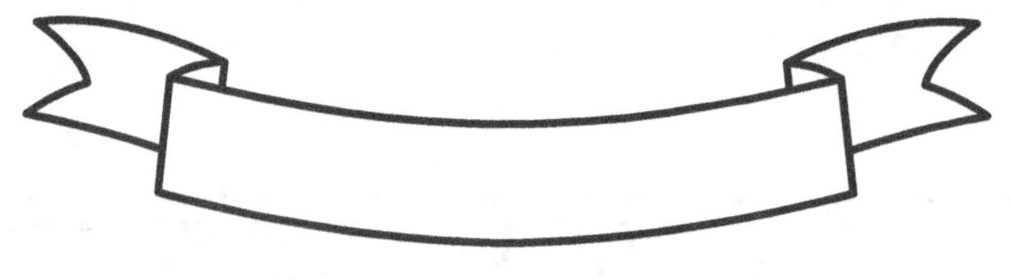

Unicorn

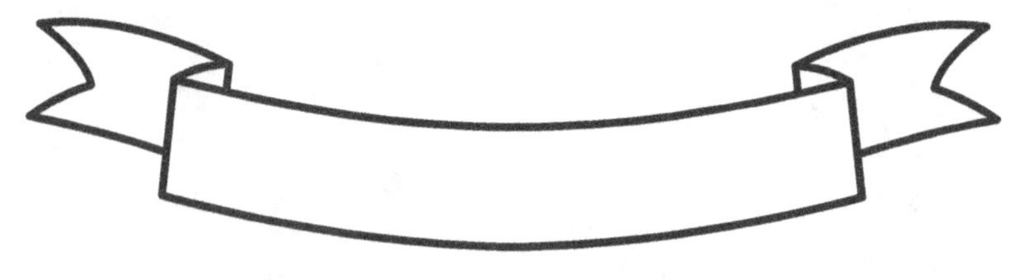

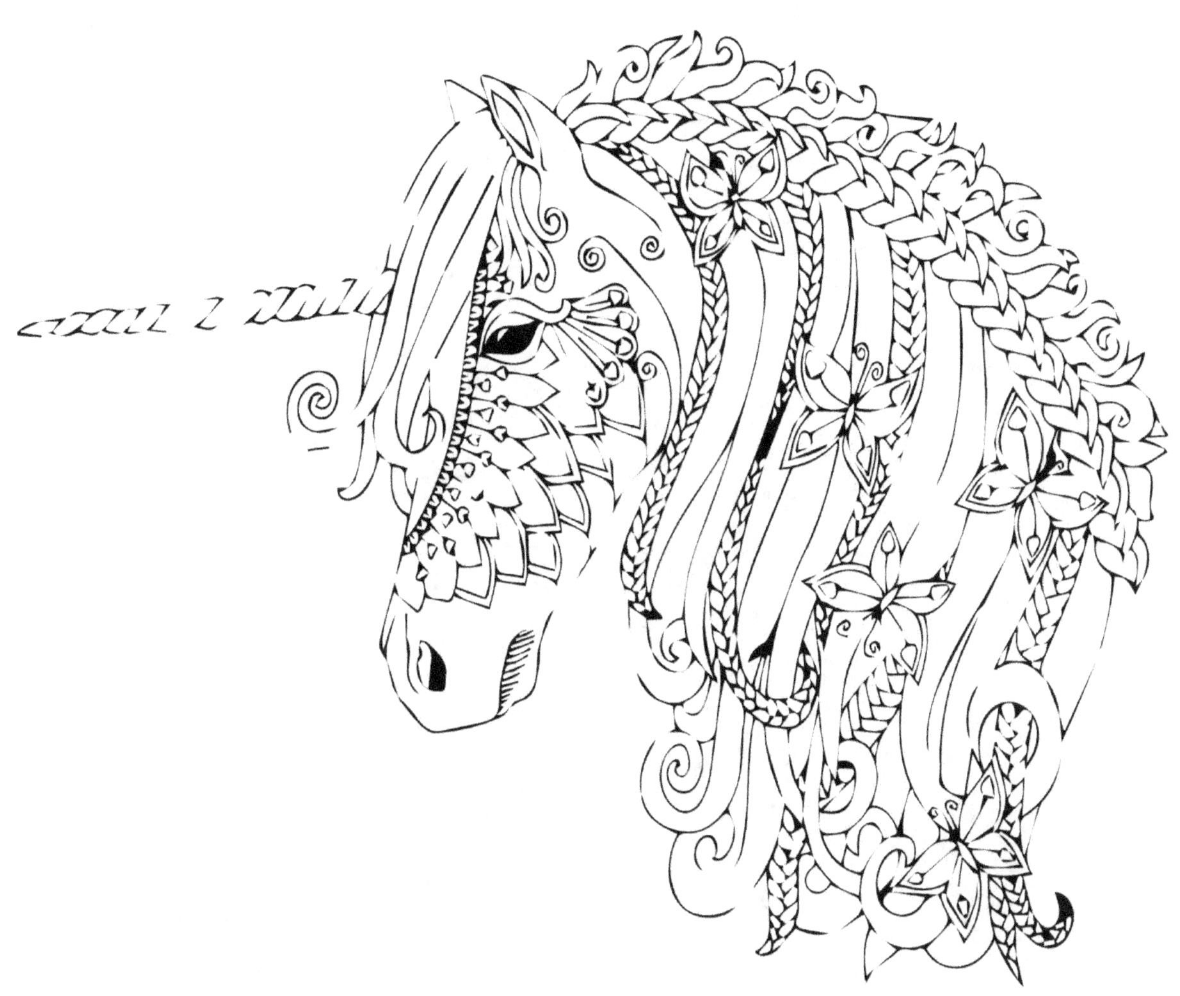

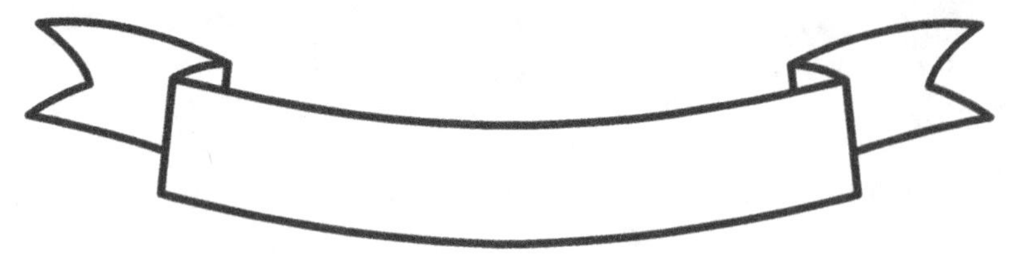

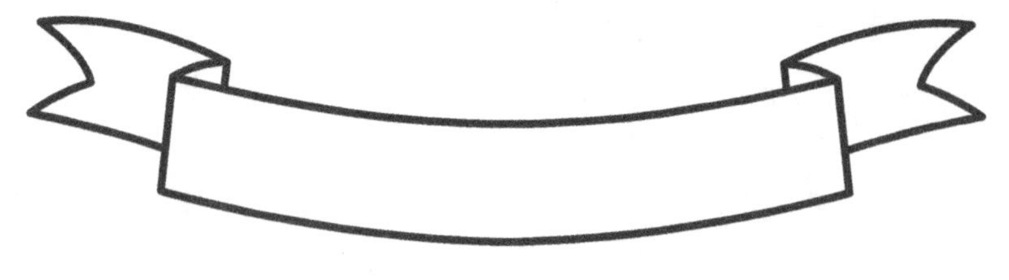

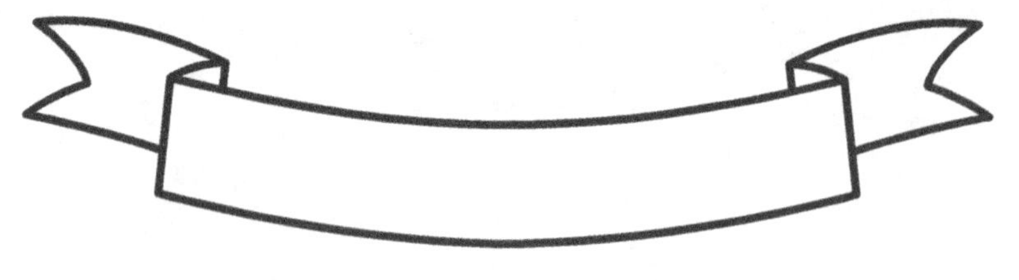

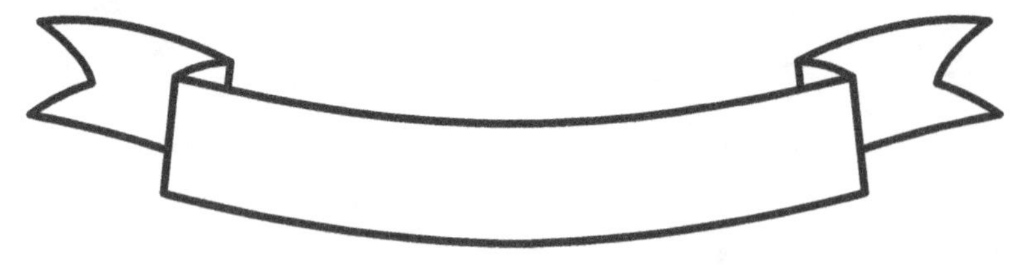

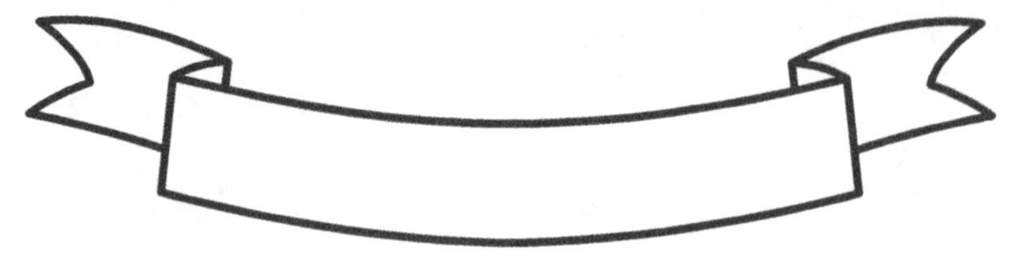